Quotes of Glory

by
Julia Kaleem

Copyright 2019©

Author	Julia Kaleem, Virginia
Publisher	DBC Publishing, Richmond, Virginia
Cover	2019 © Copyright Cover Design, DBC Publishing
ISBN-13	978-1948149150
ISBN-10	1-94814915X
Copyright Notice	2019©: The Author supports copyright, which sparks creativity, encourages diverse viewpoints, promotes free speech, and creates a vibrant and rich art culture. Thank you for buying an authorized copy of this copyrighted book and for complying with international copyright laws. You are supporting writers and allowing the artist/author to continue to publish books for every other reader to continue to enjoy. All copyrights are reserved. No part of this book, including interior design, cover design, icons, and pictures, may be reproduced or transmitted in any form, by any means (electronic, photocopying, recording, or otherwise) without the prior written permission of the copyright owner. Independent of the author's economic rights, and even after the transfer of the said rights, the author shall have the right to claim authorship of the work and to object to any distortion, modification of, and/or other derogatory action in relation to the said work that could be deemed prejudicial to the author's honor or reputation. No part of this book or images – black and white, or other renditions of images, are to be posted to any social media, Internet, and/or other digital media or platforms without prior written permission of the copyright owner.

ACKNOWLEDGMENTS

I'm so grateful and giving God all the Glory first of all. He has given me another opportunity to write my fourth book entitled: 'Quotes of Glory.' It gives me great pleasure to share to you all what God has imparted in me.

Blessings be upon my two sons, Joshua and Gershom Humbert. My grands, Malea, Shaya, Isaiah, Elijah, and Humbert (Monker).

My Church family, at Mount Olive Baptist, Centreville, Virginia, presiding Pastor, Doctor, Eugene Johnson, who has served over 25 years.

My biological family: I love you all, and a special shout out to my mother, Ruby Mitchner Franck (Florida), Samuel Gresham, Reverend Amanda Rhome, and Debra Anderson, who always have my back. I am praying as you read my fourth book that you would embrace the thoughts and lessons from the Quotes of Glory.

A REVIEW OF REVEREND JULIA KALEEM's OTHER BOOKS

I am humbled by the opportunity to share with you a few words about the author of "Quotes of Glory," written by Julia Kaleem. She's a true woman of God who loves Him and strives to follow Him in every area of her life. She and I have been through many things in the last 23 years of friendship. We are both co-laborers in spreading the Good News of the Gospel and share a friendship and sisterhood bonded by love. God has connected us through the love of family and concern for others. Her love for truth and simplicity makes her a great and easy writer to understand as she talks about God's wisdom and love for us all.

As I have already read her three other books, and now reading this fourth one, compromised of quotes given to her by the working of the Holy Spirit, which allows God who has called her to encourage and provoke you to love and further trust in him, as He enlightens and strengthens your faith.

Each quote will enable you to ponder what God is speaking to through your heart, through the working of the Holy Spirit. You will be drawn closer to God and know Him, as a loving Father. As you read each quote, allow God's Spirit to minister to you as you develop a continued and more mature relationship with him. God is using this young woman to draw us into his presence in a profound way.

Reading these quotes, I was drawn to several words of encouragement on my own continued journey in life's hopes and challenges. I pray God will allow these quotes to encourage your heart as you move forward in this journey of life as well.

I thank God and give him glory for how He is using Julia Kaleem to encourage people to continue to serve and give Him glory. May you be blessed and encouraged to continue to stand on the battlefield for God.

Reverend Amanda Rhome
Mount Olive Baptist Church,
Centreville, VA

BOOK INTRODUCTION

Praising God for his love towards me. His loving arms are amazing to me. Oh how precious is his abundantly blessing with righteousness that stirs my soul. When God allows you to rest and just listen to his voice, the words of wisdom just overflow with Quotes of Glory. As we continue to rest, it makes it easy to listen to his voice. Our day begins smoothly, and our steps are ordered by the Lord.

Many times we fail to just put him first each day because of having so much to do. 'WE SAY' … however … it is God's time. Let us put purpose in our hearts to put him first, because it is a blessing to know that God will keep us in good health, even as our soul prospereth (3 John 2, KJV).

As we lend on God first, he will show us our downfalls and make us look to him, who is the author and finisher of our faith, as it states to in God's word (Hebrew 12-2 KJV)

Lastly, these are good words expressions that you and I can focus on, during our morning, noon, and night meditations. Quotes of Glory, can also give you a double blessing, don't keep them to yourselves, just pass these words on to others and hug yourselves.

Don't be fooled by their eyes, attend to your eyes.

Kneel to truth and you can't go wrong.

Stand up and allow the wind to blow on you.

Tell yourself to leap up and not down.

⌒✗ Run, but run slowly, to stay focused.

Rub your eyes to get a clearer picture on your own situation.

⸺◡⸺ Learning is when you recognize who you are.

᚛ Live in the 'here' and not in the 'there.'

⥾ Nodding creates a sincerity of knowing.

Walking in the rain can wash away blind spots.

⊂× Don't just rule your mind change your focus.

Move straight forward and rely on your step ahead.

⌒× Life moves in every direction; be the first to grasp it tightly.

☓ The world moves outwardly, so pay attention to your inward spirit.

☓ Wondering, without a vision, holds you bound in your own tracks.

⊂× Foresee and do not just look.

Turning around in the midst of turmoil, be sure to land on your feet.

⌒✕ Stop panicking and breathe – with confidence.

⊂≍ Sleeplessness overshadows your restlessness.

⌒< Yes, your head needs to be clear, but your brain need to rest.

Think twice before you take risks because of of your doubts.

⌒× Don't let your mood play tricks on your mind.

Don't let your mouth motivate your abilities.

Sometimes your heart feels blue inside, remember, when you can breathe outwardly … that's called living.

Tiptoe on your own feet – and it will balance your mind.

Awake with motivation, not with expectations.

✝ The pure snow falls where it may; and our life falls on the pureness of the heart.

Strive for steadfastness and not shadiness.

☓ If you are going to cough up anything, let it be contagious love.

The wind moves away trash, be careful that your pile is not loaded with the silence of hatred.

Leap like a tiger, but know where to land.

Jumping up and jumping down, grounds you when you want to frown.

Start your day off with a smile, it will bring life in dead places.

Run for a cause, it will lead you to victories, as well as the unknown.

⌒⌒ Let your love be like the wind, you can feel it, but you can't grasp it, the effects of it moves on and on.

Our eye wanders, and our mind ponders; but truth is yet to be discovered in us.

⊰ Turning to the left sometimes can start a movement of corrections.

When looking upward, remember to smile a while; it's good for your next steps.

The shadows from rain, sometimes, lets us see the rainbows.

✝ Clap when things are going wrong, and you will rejoice when you come through the storms.

No matter
how high
your eyes
look, when
your eyes
see the stars,
remember on
what your
feet are
standing.

When you are lost in the wilderness, look for other's footprints to find your way.

The hands can be tools of destruction; don't forget to fold them to support your blessings.

Don't only just stand, rise above your dreams.

Let your faith be like the bird; when it is free, let it fly.

Have mercy on the simple things in life, and you will forget about strife.

⊰ Lift up your own self, in the mist of self-doubt.

Rest when you are going through your 'Test'; and you, too, will rise.

Sing and sing, victory IS in the midst, even if you don't feel it (yet).

You can break through the wells of turmoil; when you are silent, that silence brings on remembrance.

☦ Chains can be broken; but the 'brokeness' can be fixed.

When there are distractions in our lives, continue to see your blessings in the midst of storms.

Change your ways of looking at things, and you will become the change.

⌒✕ Life is where you can live, not die, in life's situations.

⌒< Love to the fullness, and that love will grow roots of caring.

Never give up on yourself, it is the only REAL you.

When your mind settles, you can get rid of fear.

Don’t just run fast, think fast, too.

⊱ Lean forward, stretch wide, and you can become un-stoppable.

Don't expect to live up to your fullness, when holes are in your bags.

Step-stones stop you from tripping on small pebbles.

Laughter makes you let go of emotions that you cannot control.

If you heart thinks hatefully, you will surely die ungrateful.

✠ Explore your positive thoughts in your mind, let them replenish your Spirit.

Pure deeds come from the depths of the soul, even when no one is looking.

᚛ Leave a period behind every negative thought; let it go, because you will not be able to start pure.

Remember that your dignity brings on greater results.

⊂⊃ Forward your love, it can take you to greater depths.

Allow yourself – to become – yourself.

God's gifts are within you; pull them out and live.

ABOUT THE AUTHOR

Julia Kaleem was born in Vero Beach, Florida and graduated from Carver High School in Montgomery, Alabama. Later, she joined the Job Corps, located in Guthrie, Oklahoma, and then joined the U.S. Army (1975), as a Telecommunication Specialist working for Military Intelligence in Primasen, Germany.

Julia has traveled all over the world, as a young girl, including to Germany, Italy, Switzerland, California, New Orleans, Kansas, Missouri, Ohio, Delaware, Georgia, Kentucky, Tennessee, Texas, Utah, Alabama, Mississippi, and Virginia.

Julia received her call into ministry in 1978, and was ordained, in 1982 under her former pastor, the late Pastor Georgianna Smith, Grace Tabernacle Church, in Fort Campbell, Kentucky. Kaleem was ordained under the leadership of Bishop Willie Dunn, Jr. (a Baptist Pastor at the time), presiding prelate of The World-Wide Gospel Church, Inc., located in Salt Lake City, Utah.

Kaleem is versed in multiple and diverse denominations. She teaches, and preaches, and officiates for weddings in Virginia. Julia has a love for all, especially the youth and elderly, on whom she leaves an impact that will not be forgotten.

Julia obtained her education at Austin Peay State University, where she majored in Business Administration and Children's Education, and later attended Strayer University, in Alexandria, Virginia, studying Business Acquisition.

In addition to this book, she has published three other books, including her poem, "Are We Really Different" in the books, "The Sketches of My Soul," and "Beyond the Horizon," (published in the National Library of Poetry). Her books can be found and purchased through: http://i2pray.com/

She believes if you would just "PAINT," (Pray And Ignore Negative Thoughts), as she has written about in her first book, you can succeed … and while succeeding … give yourself a BIG HUG and a SMILE.

CONTACT THE AUTHOR

http://i2pray.com/

jujuka1@verizon.net

ABOUT THE BOOK

This book focuses on positive thinking - which makes our life situation much easier – both physically and mentally. Thoughts of the glory of God keeps us in a positive state of mind to conquer the unknown and unforeseen influences of the negatives we encounter in life.

These quotes come from insight, and influenced by the Holy Bible, and Julia's thoughts during a period of hard times. These messages from a higher being helped her conquer the down's in her life's situations. Writing these messages, thoughts, and quotations down inspired her to share the positive messages to uplift others.

When life has you down, sometimes simple, positive messages are all you need to think about the situation. Emotionally, as well as logically, you can talk yourself into a more positive mood and viewpoint. Think, breath, reflect, and smile as you heal yourself with positivity – give yourself a hug!

www.ingramcontent.com/pod-product-compliance
Lightning Source LLC
Chambersburg PA
CBHW060850050426
42453CB00008B/925